OPENING THE COURTS OF HEAVEN TO CLEANSE YOUR BLOODLINE

Cancel the Enemy's Case Against You, Your Family, and Your Future

ROBERT HENDERSON

D DESTINY IMAGE

Copyright 2024–Destiny Image

All rights reserved. This book is protected by the copyright laws of the United States of America. This book may not be copied or reprinted for commercial gain or profit. The use of short quotations or occasional page copying for personal or group study is permitted and encouraged. Permission will be granted upon request. Unless otherwise indicated, all scripture quotations are taken from the *King James Version* of the Bible. Used by permission. All rights reserved.

All emphasis within Scripture quotations is the author's own. Please note that Destiny Image's publishing style capitalizes certain pronouns in Scripture that refer to the Father, Son, and Holy Spirit, and may differ from some publishers' styles. Take note that the name satan and related names are not capitalized. We choose not to acknowledge him, even to the point of violating grammatical rules.

Destiny Image P.O. Box 310, Shippensburg, PA 17257-0310

This book and all other Destiny Image's books are available at Christian bookstores and distributors worldwide.

For Worldwide Distribution, Printed in the U.S.A.

Reach us on the Internet: www.destinyimage.com.

ISBN 13 TP: 9798881504205

ISBN 13 eBook: 9798881504212

CONTENTS

Introduction   v

1. My Story   1
2. The Lordship of Jesus   5
3. The Reality of Generational Curses   9
4. Covenants Undone   13
5. Why Now?   17
6. Undoing Created Covenants   21
7. Repentance   25
8. Renouncing Covenants   29
9. Give It Back!   33
10. Returning Anything Gained!   36
11. Iniquity Undone   39
12. Iniquity: Interruption of God's Will   42
13. The Four Purposes of Iniquity   46
14. Silencing Voices   50
15. Signs of Curses from Our Bloodline   54
16. The Curse of Premature Death   58
17. Revoking Curses That Shorten
    Lifespans   62
18. From Defendant to Judge   66

About the Publisher   71

INTRODUCTION

෯෯

In the transformative text "Operating in the Courts of Heaven to Cleanse Your Bloodline," readers are invited to explore a profound spiritual realm where divine justice meets familial history. This book serves as a practical and theological guide to understanding and engaging with the Courts of Heaven, a concept rooted deeply in biblical teachings, specifically designed to help believers address and rectify the sins and curses that linger within their family lines.

The journey through this book is not just about learning; it's about active spiritual engagement. The author lays a foundational understanding of what the Courts of Heaven are—divine tribunals where believers can bring the grievances and curses of their bloodline before God, seeking resolution and cleansing. This process is pivotal as it is believed that unresolved sins and iniquities can hinder a believer's current life experiences, blocking blessings and perpetuating cycles of defeat.

Through a meticulous exploration of scripture, combined with compelling testimonies and personal experiences, the book elucidates how these spiritual courts operate and how one can effectively make a case before God. The readers are equipped with knowledge on how to identify the signs of curses, such as chronic illness, repeated financial failures, and unexplainable family breakdowns, all of which may suggest a deeper, unresolved spiritual issue within the bloodline.

The author emphasizes the importance of repentance and legal advocacy in the spiritual realm, teaching readers to articulate their pleas for justice and redemption eloquently. Each chapter methodically guides the reader through the process of preparing for and engaging in the Courts of Heaven, including detailed prayers and declarations aimed at renouncing the sins of the past and shutting legal doors that may have been opened through ancestral disobedience or agreements with darkness.

"Operating in the Courts of Heaven to Cleanse Your Bloodline" goes beyond mere spiritual warfare; it is an invitation to transform one's spiritual legacy. It encourages believers to not only fight for themselves but also intercede for their generations past and future. This book is a tool for empowerment—providing the knowledge to not only cleanse one's bloodline but also to secure a legacy of blessing and favor that will echo through generations.

The overarching message is one of hope and profound responsibility. It speaks to the power of the

Cross and the legal work of Jesus Christ, which not only saves us from sin but also empowers us to reclaim what the enemy has stolen from our family lines. The readers are called to rise as advocates not just for their personal healing but for the restoration of their entire lineage, setting a path of spiritual health and divine promise for the generations to come.

As we delve into the pages of this book, we are reminded of the vastness of God's court and the accessibility we have through Christ to approach with confidence. Herein lies the opportunity to step from under the shadows of generational curses into the light of scriptural promises, where each prayer and proclamation acts as a stepping stone towards profound familial redemption and divine legacy building.

CHAPTER 1

MY STORY

Bible Verse

"For I know the thoughts that I think toward you, says the Lord, thoughts of peace and not of evil, to give you a future and a hope." – Jeremiah 29:11

Introduction

This chapter serves as an intimate recounting of the trials and adversities faced by the author and his family, which ultimately led to a transformative spiritual revelation. The story is a powerful testament to the challenges of ministry, personal betrayal, and familial struggles, as well as the redemptive hope found in God's divine guidance.

Word of Wisdom

"It seemed the gates of hell had been opened against us. I was totally baffled

and perplexed over why this was happening." Robert Henderson

Main Theme

The author's story highlights the immense challenges he faced in ministry and family life, culminating in a profound encounter with God's revelation about the Courts of Heaven. It emphasizes the redemptive power of aligning with God's will and trusting Him to provide deliverance and hope, even in the most tumultuous seasons of life.

Key Points

- The author experienced an intense season of adversity following his transition from pastoral ministry to itinerant ministry.
- Slander and betrayal from trusted individuals deeply affected his reputation and finances.
- His family faced heartbreaking struggles, including divorce, addiction, and legal troubles.
- Amid the turmoil, the author began to seek deeper understanding of God's purposes and justice.
- These trials ultimately set the stage for a life-changing revelation of the Courts of Heaven.
- The chapter closes with a message of hope, affirming that deliverance is available for all who seek God.

Key Themes

- **Personal Betrayal in Ministry** The author recounts how trusted ministry colleagues turned against him, spreading false accusations and destroying his reputation. These betrayals highlighted the pain of broken relationships and the spiritual battles faced by those in leadership.
- **Family Struggles and Heartbreak** The chapter shares the author's heartache over his sons' trials—one son battling addiction and legal troubles, and another facing a painful divorce and separation from his child. These stories reveal the deep emotional toll of familial challenges.
- **Financial Loss and Unforeseen Consequences** Trusting others with financial decisions led to devastating outcomes, including the loss of home equity and financial security. These hardships underscore the far-reaching consequences of misplaced trust.
- **The Dark Night of the Soul** In the midst of these trials, the author struggled to make sense of the chaos, feeling abandoned and confused. This period of desperation ultimately led him to seek God more fervently for answers.
- **The Revelation of the Courts of Heaven** The overwhelming challenges served as a catalyst for the author's understanding of the Courts of Heaven, a spiritual framework for addressing generational curses and legal rights in the

spiritual realm. This revelation brought renewed hope and purpose.

Conclusion

The author's story serves as a reminder that even in the darkest moments, God is at work to bring restoration and revelation. The trials and betrayals, while painful, became the backdrop for discovering spiritual truths that can transform lives. This chapter invites readers to trust in God's justice and seek His guidance for overcoming their own challenges.

CHAPTER 2

THE LORDSHIP OF JESUS

Bible Verse

"And being found in appearance as a man, He humbled Himself and became obedient to the point of death, even the death of the cross. Therefore God also has highly exalted Him and given Him the name which is above every name." – Philippians 2:8-9

Introduction

This chapter explores the necessity of submitting to the Lordship of Jesus in every area of life. Drawing from personal experiences, biblical insights, and practical examples, it emphasizes the importance of obedience, digging deep into faith, and maintaining a mindset of continual spiritual growth.

Word of Wisdom

"We don't just do lip service to His

Lordship, but actually submit all things to Him and His authority." Robert Henderson

Main Theme

The chapter stresses that Jesus' Lordship must be more than a declaration; it requires action, obedience, and a steadfast commitment to aligning one's life with His Word. This submission brings stability and favor, even amidst life's challenges, and grants believers legal standing in the Courts of Heaven.

Key Points

- Submitting to Jesus as Lord requires action, not just words.
- A firm foundation in Christ enables believers to endure life's storms.
- Obedience to God's instructions speaks on behalf of believers in the spiritual realm.
- Digging deep into faith reveals the true foundation of one's life in Christ.
- Building a life under Christ's Lordship is an ongoing process, not a completed act.
- Sacrificial obedience unlocks divine blessings and spiritual authority.

Key Themes

- **Authentic Submission to Jesus' Lordship** True submission requires aligning every area of life with His authority, not merely acknowledging Him with words. Obedience to His commands transforms believers into steadfast witnesses of His grace and sovereignty.
- **The Importance of a Firm Foundation** A life built on the Rock of Christ can withstand the trials and storms of life. This foundation is laid by hearing and obeying His Word, ensuring spiritual resilience and stability.
- **Obedience as a Legal Testimony** Acts of obedience, such as supporting God's purposes or following His instructions, carry weight in the Courts of Heaven. These actions not only honor God but also speak on behalf of believers, granting them spiritual authority.
- **Continuous Spiritual Growth** Building under Christ's Lordship requires a mindset of perpetual growth and refinement. Believers must remain open to the Holy Spirit's work, allowing God to complete His good work in them.
- **Digging Deep to Discover the Rock** The process of digging deep signifies an intentional pursuit of Christ through prayer, study, and revelation. This effort leads to an unshakable faith, rooted in the knowledge of who Jesus is.

Conclusion

The Lordship of Jesus demands a life of obedience, continual growth, and intentional alignment with His will. By building on the Rock, believers can face any storm and fulfill their divine purposes. As the author concludes, making Jesus Lord of all brings spiritual stability, favor, and a place of authority in the Courts of Heaven.

CHAPTER 3

THE REALITY OF
GENERATIONAL CURSES

Bible Verse

"Christ has redeemed us from the curse of the law, having become a curse for us (for it is written, 'Cursed is everyone who hangs on a tree')." – Galatians 3:13

Introduction

This chapter explores the controversial topic of generational curses and their relevance under New Testament grace. It highlights the necessity of understanding scriptural truths about bloodline iniquity, repentance, and the legal authority believers possess through Christ to annul curses.

Word of Wisdom

"Without the person of the Holy Spirit, nothing Jesus did on the cross would have application in our lives."
Robert Henderson

Main Theme

The chapter addresses the biblical and spiritual reality of generational curses, asserting that believers must cooperate with the Holy Spirit to revoke the enemy's legal claims. It emphasizes the importance of repentance, the role of scripture, and the execution of Christ's finished work to experience freedom from bloodline iniquity.

Key Points

- Generational curses are legal claims the enemy uses to hinder success and future potential.
- The Old Testament remains foundational for understanding New Testament grace and the work of Christ.
- The Holy Spirit implements the legal work of the cross, enabling believers to apply its benefits.
- Repentance is key to nullifying bloodline iniquity and freeing oneself from its consequences.
- Full deliverance from curses will occur in the millennium reign of Christ, but believers can experience freedom now through faith and action.
- Proper understanding and application of scripture are essential for overcoming generational curses.

Key Themes

- **The Continuing Relevance of the Old Testament** The Old Testament is foundational for New Testament teachings, providing insight into God's laws and promises. Dismissing its significance undermines the depth of scriptural truth and hinders believers from understanding the work of the cross.

- **The Role of the Holy Spirit** The Holy Spirit executes the legal work of the cross, making it applicable in believers' lives. Cooperation with the Spirit is essential for annulling curses and experiencing the full benefits of Christ's sacrifice.

- **The Legal Nature of Curses and the Work of the Cross** Curses represent legal rights for the enemy to disrupt lives, but Christ's sacrifice rendered a verdict against these claims. Believers must enforce this verdict through prayer and spiritual action to experience freedom.

- **The Importance of Repentance** Repentance is critical for breaking generational curses and removing the power of bloodline iniquity. By aligning with God's desire for freedom, believers can revoke legal claims and secure their divine destiny.

- **The Process of Full Redemption** While Christ's work on the cross provides the basis for freedom, believers must actively engage in the spiritual process to apply it. Full redemption from curses will manifest during Christ's millennial reign, but partial deliverance is achievable now through faith and obedience.

Conclusion

Generational curses are a real spiritual challenge, but through the power of the Holy Spirit and the finished work of the cross, believers can overcome them. By understanding the significance of scripture, repenting for bloodline iniquity, and cooperating with the Spirit, Christians can experience freedom and fulfillment in God's promises. As the author asserts, *"We can stand in the Courts of Heaven and see every legal claim against us removed."*

CHAPTER 4

COVENANTS UNDONE

Bible Verse

"The blood of sprinkling that speaks better things than that of Abel." – Hebrews 12:24

Introduction

This chapter recounts the author's life-changing experience of discovering and breaking a demonic covenant hidden in his bloodline. It highlights the spiritual significance of ancestral agreements, the power of repentance, and the transformative impact of aligning oneself with the covenant of Christ through prayer.

Word of Wisdom

"I had been standing in the Courts of Heaven and was undoing the covenant claims the devil had used to harass my life and destiny." Robert Henderson

. . .

Main Theme

The chapter emphasizes the necessity of addressing ancestral covenants and legal rights the enemy may hold in our bloodlines. It reveals how prayer and repentance can annul these covenants, releasing believers from spiritual bondage and aligning them with God's purposes.

Key Points

- The author faced severe attacks despite living under the Lordship of Jesus and seeking God diligently.
- A prophetic session revealed a demonic covenant in the author's bloodline with a demon named Parax.
- This covenant granted the enemy legal rights to bring destruction and hinder the author's family and destiny.
- Through targeted prayers of repentance and renunciation, the covenant with Parax was annulled.
- The author discovered that the power of the blood of Jesus overrides any legal claim of the enemy.
- Breaking the covenant resulted in significant spiritual breakthroughs and restored alignment with God's promises.

Key Themes

- **The Reality of Ancestral Covenants**
  Hidden agreements made by ancestors can grant the enemy legal rights to hinder descendants. These covenants, often unknown to individuals, must be exposed and addressed through spiritual discernment and prayer.
- **The Power of Prayer and Repentance**
  The author's prayer of repentance, renunciation, and reliance on Christ's blood effectively annulled the demonic covenant. This demonstrates that aligning with Christ's covenant is a powerful weapon against spiritual oppression.
- **The Authority of the Blood of Jesus**
  The blood of Jesus speaks on behalf of believers in the Courts of Heaven, nullifying the claims of the enemy. This divine provision offers a pathway to freedom from generational strongholds.
- **Legal Standing in the Courts of Heaven** The session revealed the spiritual reality of standing in the Courts of Heaven to undo legal claims of the enemy. This process emphasizes the importance of addressing spiritual legalities through faith and prayer.
- **Breakthroughs After Annulment**
  Once the covenant was broken, the author experienced a shift in his spiritual journey, with delays and attacks vanishing. This underscores the significance of dealing with spiritual hindrances to walk fully in God's promises.

Conclusion

The author's discovery and annulment of a demonic covenant in his bloodline became a turning point in his spiritual journey. By relying on the blood of Jesus and engaging in intentional prayer and repentance, he overcame legal claims that had hindered his life and family. This chapter serves as a reminder that freedom and breakthrough are available when believers address spiritual legalities and align fully with Christ's covenant.

CHAPTER 5

WHY NOW?

Bible Verse

"Your eyes saw my substance, being yet unformed. And in Your book they all were written, the days fashioned for me, when as yet there were none of them." – Psalm 139:16

Introduction

This chapter explores the sudden onset of spiritual attacks that coincided with the author stepping into a greater kingdom purpose. It delves into the reality of spiritual opposition, the importance of destiny written in heaven's books, and the role of the Courts of Heaven in nullifying legal claims of the enemy.

Word of Wisdom

"When the Lord from His council decided to make me His messenger concerning the Courts of Heaven, the devil

commissioned a seeking out of a legal right to destroy me." Robert Henderson

Main Theme

The chapter emphasizes that stepping into a greater destiny often triggers spiritual opposition. However, through intercession, repentance, and understanding the legalities of the spiritual realm, believers can nullify the enemy's claims and fully embrace God's purpose.

Key Points

- Spiritual attacks intensified when the author began pursuing a global kingdom impact.
- The devil searches for legal rights to oppose believers, often exploiting hidden ancestral agreements.
- God has a divine book for each person's destiny, which must be opened for their purpose to be fulfilled.
- Intercession and alignment with God's will are crucial for accessing and fulfilling one's heavenly mandate.
- Biblical figures like Isaiah and Job demonstrate how navigating spiritual challenges leads to victory and vindication.
- The Courts of Heaven provide a framework for removing the enemy's legal claims and advancing in God's plans.

Key Themes

- **The Trigger of Spiritual Opposition**
Greater kingdom impact often provokes
the enemy to search for legal grounds to
hinder believers. The author's shift from
local ministry to global influence
intensified attacks as the enemy sought to
derail his destiny.

- **Destiny Written in Heaven's Books**
Every believer has a unique purpose
documented in God's heavenly books.
These books must be opened through
intercession and obedience to align with
and fulfill divine purposes.

- **The Devil as a Legal Opponent** The
enemy acts as a prosecuting attorney,
seeking legal rights to disrupt believers'
lives. Hidden ancestral agreements, like
the covenant with Parax, can become tools
of spiritual sabotage.

- **Biblical Examples of Spiritual
Navigation** Figures like Isaiah and Job
illustrate the necessity of navigating
spiritual trials through obedience and
repentance. These challenges refine
believers and ultimately position them for
greater kingdom assignments.

- **Victory Through the Courts of
Heaven** Engaging the Courts of Heaven
allows believers to revoke legal claims of
the enemy, ensuring God's will prevails.
The author's victory highlights the
transformative power of this spiritual
process.

Conclusion

The author's journey illustrates that stepping into a larger kingdom role often brings heightened spiritual warfare. By understanding the Courts of Heaven, engaging in intercession, and aligning with God's will, believers can overcome the enemy's tactics and fulfill their divine purpose. As the author reminds, *"May You find in me a humble servant desiring to complete all You ordained from the books of heaven."*

CHAPTER 6

UNDOING CREATED COVENANTS

Bible Verse

"For He made Him who knew no sin to be sin for us, that we might become the righteousness of God in Him." – 2 Corinthians 5:21

Introduction

This chapter delves into the concept of covenants made with demonic powers, exploring their origins, the biblical basis for their existence, and the spiritual mechanisms through which they can be undone. It emphasizes the power of Jesus' sacrifice as the ultimate trade to nullify such covenants.

Word of Wisdom

"We undo the trades we have made with satan through agreeing with the trade of Jesus for us." Robert Henderson

Main Theme

The focus of the chapter is on understanding and reversing the effects of demonic covenants created through trades or agreements, whether done knowingly or unknowingly, by our ancestors or ourselves.

Key Points

- Demonic covenants may be created for protection or favor but bind descendants to spiritual oppression.
- Such covenants are often established through trades, which can be offerings or other forms of agreement with demonic entities.
- Jesus' death on the cross represents the ultimate trade, offering His righteousness in exchange for our sin and bondage.
- Spiritual freedom from demonic covenants involves recognizing these agreements and renouncing them in the Courts of Heaven.
- The intercession and repentance of believers are crucial for activating the power of Christ's trade on the cross to annul demonic agreements.
- Engaging in spiritual warfare and understanding heavenly trading principles are vital for maintaining spiritual authority and inheritance.

Key Themes

- **The Historical Basis for Demonic Covenants** Early biblical leaders sometimes entered into covenants with demonic forces for perceived earthly benefits. These agreements are spiritual and have lasting consequences that can affect future generations until they are spiritually addressed and undone.

- **Understanding Trades and Covenants** Trading in the spiritual realm involves exchanges that can either align with God's purposes or demonic intentions. Identifying these trades helps in understanding how covenants with demonic entities are formed and how they can be dismantled.

- **Jesus as the Ultimate Trade** Jesus' sacrifice on the cross is portrayed as the perfect trade, offering His purity and righteousness in exchange for our sins and the covenants formed from them. This trade is the foundation for all deliverance from demonic agreements.

- **The Role of Intercession in Undoing Covenants** Intercession and repentance play a critical role in accessing the benefits of Jesus' sacrifice. Believers must actively engage in these spiritual disciplines to invoke the power of the cross against demonic covenants.

- **Legal Proceedings in the Spiritual Realm** The concept of the Courts of Heaven is instrumental in understanding how believers can argue against demonic claims legally. By presenting the sacrifice of Jesus as evidence, believers can annul wrongful covenants and reclaim their spiritual heritage.

Conclusion

Undoing Created Covenants emphasizes the necessity of understanding spiritual trading and covenant-making to reclaim the life and destiny ordained by God. Through the power of Jesus' ultimate trade on the cross, believers can overturn any demonic agreements affecting their lives and ensure their actions align with the righteousness granted through Christ's sacrifice. The chapter challenges believers to be vigilant about their spiritual engagements and to utilize their authority in Christ to maintain freedom from any legal claims of the enemy.

CHAPTER 7

REPENTANCE

Bible Verse

"But if we walk in the light, as he is in the light, we have fellowship with one another, and the blood of Jesus, his Son, purifies us from all sin." – 1 John 1:7

Introduction

This chapter explores the profound importance of repentance, both personally and ancestrally, in overcoming legal claims the devil may hold due to covenants made with demonic powers. It underscores the transformative power of true repentance in aligning with God's purposes and hastening the ultimate judgment against satanic forces.

Word of Wisdom

"Repentance allows us to recover ourselves from the powers of darkness according to 2 Timothy 2:24-26."

Main Theme

Repentance is critical in revoking any legal claims against us by demonic forces, aiding in the fulfillment of our divine destinies and hastening the end of satanic influence on earth.

Key Points

• Repentance is essential for annulling demonic covenants and claims.

• True repentance involves a deep emotional and spiritual recognition of sin's impact on our relationship with God.

• It is not just about personal sin but also includes ancestral sins that may affect one's destiny.

• Repentance leads to a liberation from satanic snares, allowing believers to fulfill their God-given destinies.

• The process of repentance activates the power of Christ's sacrificial blood, speaking on our behalf in the spiritual realm.

• Through repentance, believers can significantly influence the spiritual timeline, including the return of Christ and the final judgment of Satan.

Key Themes

• **Nature and Necessity of Repentance**
Repentance involves a profound
recognition and turning away from sin,

both personally and ancestrally. It's not merely an emotional response but a strategic and spiritual action that revokes the enemy's claims.

- **Impact on Personal and Ancestral Legacies** By addressing both personal and ancestral sins, repentance cleanses our spiritual lineage, freeing us and future generations from the repercussions of past covenants with demonic forces.
- **Spiritual and Eschatological Implications** The act of repentance has both immediate spiritual benefits and eschatological implications, accelerating the fulfillment of divine prophecies and hastening the end times as outlined in biblical prophecy.
- **Mechanics of Repentance in the Spiritual Realm** Repentance grants us access to the Courts of Heaven where legal arguments against demonic claims can be nullified, based on the advocacy of Jesus Christ and His redemptive work on the cross.
- **Catalyst for Divine Destiny** As believers engage in genuine repentance, they unlock their divine destinies, overcoming spiritual barriers and enabling the full realization of their roles in God's overarching plan.

Conclusion

Repentance is a pivotal chapter that illuminates the power of repentance in disarming the legal maneuvers of satanic forces against believers. Through heartfelt repentance, believers reclaim their divine heritage and accelerate the fulfillment of God's kingdom on earth, contributing directly to the ultimate defeat of satanic forces and the establishment of eternal justice.

CHAPTER 8

RENOUNCING COVENANTS

Bible Verse

"Therefore, since we have this ministry, as we have received mercy, we do not lose heart. But we have renounced the hidden things of shame, not walking in craftiness nor handling the word of God deceitfully, but by manifestation of the truth commending ourselves to every man's conscience in the sight of God." – 2 Corinthians 4:1-2

Introduction

This chapter emphasizes the power of renouncing demonic covenants after repentance, detailing how such declarations help believers sever ties with negative spiritual influences and reclaim their divine authority and destiny.

Word of Wisdom

"Our words carry great power in the

spirit world. When we use them to re-nounce agreements and covenants with demons, we are separating ourselves from their influence and effect." Robert Henderson

Main Theme

The renunciation of demonic covenants is a crucial step following repentance, essential for breaking the adversary's claims and walking in the fullness of one's spiritual authority and freedom.

Key Points

• Renouncing involves a verbal disowning of demonic covenants.

• It is a declaration that these covenants have no power over the believer.

• This act must follow repentance to fully break the ties.

• Words used in renunciation carry significant spiritual authority.

• Renunciation can be recognized in the Courts of Heaven.

• It effectively separates believers from past spiritual claims.

Key Themes

- **Power and Importance of Words** The words spoken by a believer have the power to effect change in the spiritual realm. Using these words to renounce demonic influences asserts one's authority over such powers and initiates spiritual liberation.
- **Spiritual Authority Through Renunciation** Renouncing demonic covenants allows believers to exercise their God-given authority, breaking ties with past agreements and claiming freedom from demonic oppression.
- **Role of Faith in Spiritual Declarations** Faith plays a crucial role in the effectiveness of renouncing words; without faith, these declarations might not reach their full spiritual potential, underscoring the need for a strong belief in the power of spoken words.
- **Legal Aspects in the Spirit Realm** Just as in the physical world, the spiritual realm operates under legalities where words used in renunciation can have legal standing in spiritual courts, effectively nullifying past agreements with demonic entities.
- **Continuous Process and Warfare** The process of renunciation is not a one-time event but part of ongoing spiritual warfare. Believers must continuously assert their authority and remain vigilant against any new or lingering claims from the enemy.

Conclusion

Renouncing Covenants profoundly explains how after repentance, believers must vocally disown and dismiss all ties with demonic powers. This renunciation is powerful and liberating, enabling individuals to step fully into their divine destinies free from past encumbrances. By understanding and utilizing their spiritual authority, believers can maintain their freedom and influence the spiritual realm positively, hastening the fulfillment of God's kingdom purposes.

CHAPTER 9

GIVE IT BACK!

Bible Verse

"Every good gift and every perfect gift is from above, and comes down from the Father of lights, with whom there is no variation or shadow of turning." – James 1:17

Introduction

This chapter explores the necessity of relinquishing any gains perceived to have been obtained through demonic covenants to fully free oneself from their binds and legally restore one's standing in the spiritual realm.

Word of Wisdom

"When I know how good God is, I will have no problem in letting go of what demons might claim to have provided."
Robert Henderson

Main Theme

Renouncing and returning gains from demonic covenants is essential to breaking free from their claims and restoring one's spiritual authority and blessings truly from God.

Key Points

• Gains from demonic sources must be returned to ensure full spiritual liberation.

• Trust in God's goodness is essential when relinquishing such gains.

• The devil's claims are legally voided through the act of giving back.

• Spiritual authority is reclaimed by renouncing demonic ties.

• Legal actions in the spirit are necessary to counter demonic claims.

• Renunciation leads to a restoration of true blessings from God.

Key Themes

• **Necessity of Returning Demonic Gains** Anything gained through demonic covenants must be returned to sever ties and disclaim any associated benefits, acknowledging that true blessings come solely from God.

• **Spiritual and Legal Implications** Not returning these gains allows demonic entities legal grounds to claim continued influence or control; thus, renunciation is both a spiritual and a legally necessary act to regain freedom.

- **Restoration of Divine Blessings** Upon renouncing and returning demonic gains, one can fully embrace and recognize the true blessings that come from God alone, devoid of any impurity or manipulation from evil sources.
- **Impact on Generational Blessings** The act of giving back influences not only the individual but also has ramifications on their lineage, protecting future generations from the consequences of demonic agreements.
- **Faith and Trust in God's Provision** A deep trust in God's goodness and the integrity of His provisions is crucial when discarding the alleged benefits from demonic sources, reinforcing one's reliance on divine rather than corrupt sources.

Conclusion

Give It Back! articulates the importance of not only renouncing but also actively returning any perceived gains from demonic covenants to fully liberate oneself and restore rightful blessings. This action reinforces a believer's commitment to God's sovereignty and purity of His gifts, ensuring that their spiritual journey and lineage are free from demonic claims and are aligned with divine truth and blessings.

CHAPTER 10

RETURNING ANYTHING GAINED!

Bible Verse

"I will hedge up your way with thorns, And wall her in, So that she cannot find her paths." – Hosea 2:6

Introduction

This chapter discusses the remaining four of seven potential consequences for not returning gains obtained through demonic covenants, emphasizing the need for spiritual and legal rectification to restore blessings and opportunities intended by God.

Word of Wisdom

"Only when we fully annul any demonic covenant by giving back what they claim we gained will that covenant be revoked." Robert Henderson

Main Theme

The necessity of returning gains from demonic sources to prevent spiritual and material losses and to unlock God's intended blessings and prosperity.

Key Points

• Unreturned demonic gains can block paths to success.

• Demonic claims can be legally countered through spiritual restitution.

• Giving back ill-gotten gains restores opportunities and prosperity.

• Spiritual authority and blessings are reclaimed by rejecting demonic ties.

• Legal actions in the spirit realm are essential to overcoming demonic claims.

Key Themes

- **Blocked Paths to Success** Failing to return demonic gains can result in blocked opportunities and thwarted success, as spiritual legality allows demonic forces to hinder one's progress.
- **Restoration of Opportunities** By returning these gains and renouncing demonic covenants, one can restore their path to prosperity and success, aligning with the biblical promise of a prosperous future as seen in Joshua 1:8.
- **Reclaiming Spiritual Authority** The act of returning gains is both a

renunciation of demonic influence and a proclamation of reliance on God's provision, which reclaims spiritual authority and divine protection.

- **Legal Implications in the Spiritual Realm** Demonic covenants hold legal weight in the spiritual realm; therefore, actively renouncing these covenants and returning any associated gains nullifies these legal bindings.
- **Comprehensive Spiritual Restoration** Complete spiritual restoration requires thorough legal and spiritual actions—repentance, renunciation, and the physical act of returning gains—to fully align with God's laws and blessings.

Conclusion

Returning Anything Gained! underlines the critical action of giving back illicit gains to sever ties with demonic influences fully. This spiritual and legal process is essential for removing barriers to success, restoring lost opportunities, and ensuring the flow of God's intended blessings into one's life and lineage.

CHAPTER 11

INIQUITY UNDONE

Bible Verse

"You shall not bow down to them nor serve them. For I, the Lord your God, am a jealous God, visiting the iniquity of the fathers upon the children to the third and fourth generations of those who hate Me." – Exodus 20:4-5

Introduction

This chapter explores the concept of iniquity within bloodlines as a legal basis for satanic claims against individuals and families, emphasizing the necessity of addressing these spiritual liabilities to realize God's promises fully.

Word of Wisdom

"The fight in any court is about what is going to be allowed in as evidence."
Robert Henderson

Main Theme

The critical need to address and rectify ancestral iniquities to prevent demonic legal claims and ensure spiritual and generational freedom.

Key Points

• Iniquity refers to ancestral sins that affect descendants up to four generations.

• Legal claims by Satan based on iniquity can hinder God's promises.

• Addressing iniquity involves specific, focused repentance.

• Limiting spiritual scrutiny to four generations aligns with biblical directives.

• Effective prayer requires adherence to scriptural boundaries to avoid empowering demonic claims.

Key Themes

• **Nature of Iniquity** Iniquity is distinct from other sins due to its ancestral character and its potential to shape personal tendencies and familial legacies. The rectification of iniquities is crucial for breaking legal claims satan might use to obstruct an individual's divine destiny.

• **Biblical Limitation on Iniquity's Impact** The Bible restricts the impact of ancestral sins to three to four generations, which provides a feasible scope for spiritual interventions. This limitation is

40

crucial for making the process of cleansing one's bloodline achievable and preventing undue satanic advantage.

- **Repentance and Legal Precedents** Focused repentance and understanding of spiritual legalities are necessary to effectively counteract the claims made by demonic forces based on iniquity. Addressing these issues directly in prayer supports spiritual liberation and blessing.
- **Avoidance of Endless Genealogies** Avoiding endless genealogies and focusing on the biblically prescribed generational limit prevents unnecessary spiritual conflicts and simplifies the process of bloodline cleansing. This practice aligns with Paul's warnings and helps maintain clear and directed spiritual warfare.
- **Practical Outcomes of Addressing Iniquity** Addressing iniquities not only clears legal obstacles in the spiritual realm but also restores the individual's capacity to fully embrace and realize God's promises. It repairs one's spiritual authority and potential for generational blessings.

Conclusion

Iniquity Undone emphasizes the power and necessity of addressing ancestral sins to thwart satanic legal claims that hinder personal and generational blessings. By aligning prayer and repentance with scriptural directives, believers can secure their spiritual inheritance and facilitate generational redemption.

CHAPTER 12

INIQUITY:
INTERRUPTION OF
GOD'S WILL

Bible Verse

"For the Lord has poured out on you the spirit of deep sleep, and has closed your eyes, namely, the prophets; and He has covered your heads, namely, the seers." – Isaiah 29:10

Introduction

This chapter delves into the profound impact of unaddressed iniquity within our bloodlines, which can significantly disrupt God's intended purposes for our lives, and explores strategies to overcome these spiritual obstacles.

Word of Wisdom

"Worship will open our books." Robert Henderson

Main Theme

Addressing the spiritual and generational impact of iniquity, focusing on the necessity of engaging in heavenly court battles to realign with God's predetermined plans for our lives as inscribed in heavenly books.

Key Points

• Iniquity has a deep-rooted influence that can shape our spiritual identity and destiny.

• The Holy Spirit and iniquity are in conflict, both trying to mold us.

• Our lives and destinies are prewritten in heavenly books.

• Understanding and addressing iniquity is crucial for fulfilling our divine purpose.

• Worship is a powerful tool in combating the sealing of our spiritual books.

• Real worship involves seeking God, opening our treasures, and hearing from Him.

Key Themes

• **Conflict Between the Holy Spirit and Iniquity** The chapter emphasizes the ongoing battle between the Holy Spirit's influence and the iniquity rooted in our bloodlines. While the Holy Spirit aims to mold us according to God's original plan for us, iniquity seeks to divert and distort this divine blueprint.

- **Significance of Heavenly Books** Our destinies, including our strengths, callings, and lifespans, are documented in heavenly books, which the Holy Spirit references to guide us towards our God-given purpose. These books are essential for understanding what God has planned for us and need to be "opened" for us to access this knowledge.

- **Impact of Sealed Books** Sealed books result in a lack of prophetic vision, causing frustration and spiritual stagnation. The sealing of these books prevents us from accessing knowledge of our divine destiny, which can lead to a life not aligned with God's purposes.

- **Role of Worship in Accessing Divine Plans** Engaging in true worship plays a crucial role in unsealing the books that contain our divine mandates. Worship not only brings us closer to God but also acts as a key to unlocking the sealed books, allowing us to receive prophetic revelation and guidance.

- **Legal Battles in the Courts of Heaven** The chapter outlines the necessity of presenting our cases in the heavenly courts to contend against the claims made by iniquity. By legally addressing these claims, we can nullify their effects and align ourselves more closely with the intentions written in our heavenly books.

Conclusion

Iniquity: Interruption of God's Will serves as a compelling guide on the importance of recognizing and overcoming the spiritual hindrances caused by ancestral iniquity. Through focused prayer, worship, and heavenly legal proceedings, believers can unlock their prophetic destinies and adhere more closely to God's original blueprint for their lives.

CHAPTER 13

THE FOUR PURPOSES OF INIQUITY

Bible Verse

"If we confess our sins, He is faithful and just to forgive us our sins and to cleanse us from all unrighteousness." —1 John 1:9 (NKJV)

Introduction

T his chapter delves into the spiritual impact of unaddressed iniquity, exploring how it provides Satan with legal rights to oppose our destiny and God's purposes in our lives. Using biblical examples such as Peter, Isaiah, and David, the author illustrates how iniquity operates through temptation, identity distortion, destiny destruction, and legal accusations, and offers practical steps for breaking its hold through repentance and divine intervention.

Word of Wisdom

"When we cleanse our bloodline and revoke the legal claim of iniquity against

us, the inner idea of who we are changes."
Robert Henderson

Main Theme

Iniquity, if left unchecked, serves as a legal and spiritual barrier to fulfilling God's plans for our lives. Understanding its operations and seeking deliverance through the Courts of Heaven is essential to walk freely in our God-ordained destiny.

Key Points

• Iniquity gives Satan legal rights to tempt us, leading to sin and spiritual bondage.

• It distorts our identity, shaping how we perceive ourselves based on past sin and bloodline issues.

• Iniquity can destroy destinies by redirecting us away from God's purposes.

• Broken covenants and unrepented sins in the bloodline can bring consequences like spiritual famine or financial lack.

• Repentance and seeking God's intervention can annul the legal rights of iniquity in our lives.

• Victory over iniquity enables believers to fulfill their divine calling without spiritual hindrances.

Key Themes

- **Temptation Through Iniquity:** Iniquity enables Satan to exploit our weaknesses and tempt us in areas where our bloodline has previously faltered. This creates a cycle of sin and accusation, leaving us spiritually bound unless broken by divine intervention.
- **Identity Distortion:** Iniquity shapes how we see ourselves, often reinforcing guilt, shame, and unworthiness. By addressing iniquity, we can align our self-perception with God's truth and walk confidently in our identity as His children.
- **Destruction of Destiny:** Left unaddressed, iniquity can lead to life-altering consequences, redirecting us from God's intended path. The author shares personal and biblical examples of individuals whose destinies were either fulfilled or thwarted depending on their response to iniquity.
- **Legal Accusations in the Courts of Heaven:** Satan uses unrepented sins and broken covenants as legal grounds to hinder our spiritual progress. By engaging in repentance and prayer, believers can annul these accusations and revoke the enemy's rights.
- **The Power of Repentance:** Through genuine repentance, the iniquity in our bloodline can be cleansed, breaking strongholds and silencing the voice of the accuser. This process restores freedom and aligns us with God's purposes.

Conclusion

Unresolved iniquity can have far-reaching effects on our spiritual lives, identity, and destiny. However, by understanding its operations and applying the principles of repentance and intercession, we can silence its voice and remove its grip. With God's intervention, we are empowered to fulfill our divine assignments, free from spiritual bondage.

CHAPTER 14

SILENCING VOICES

Bible Verse

"No weapon formed against you shall prosper, and every tongue which rises against you in judgment You shall condemn." —Isaiah 54:17 (NKJV)

Introduction

This chapter focuses on silencing the spiritual voices of accusation that oppose believers in the Courts of Heaven. These voices, led by Satan, can hinder breakthroughs, limit destinies, and perpetuate curses through legal accusations based on sin and iniquity. By understanding the principles of spiritual authority and the power of Jesus' blood, believers can silence these voices and reclaim freedom and victory in their lives and bloodlines.

Word of Wisdom

"If I can silence the myriad of voices

in the spirit world against me, I can get breakthrough." Robert Henderson

Main Theme

The spiritual accusations made by Satan and his forces act as significant barriers to the manifestation of God's purposes. Believers are called to silence these voices using their authority in Christ, the power of His blood, and the righteousness they inherit through faith.

Key Points

• Satan, as the accuser, continually presents cases against believers in the Courts of Heaven.

• These accusations draw from personal sins and generational iniquities, giving legal grounds for spiritual interference.

• Silencing these voices through faith in Jesus' blood removes the power of these accusations.

• Isaiah 54:17 teaches that believers have the heritage and authority to condemn any tongue raised against them.

• The gift of righteousness empowers believers to overcome accusations and reign in life.

• Cleansing bloodlines through the testimony of Jesus' blood silences accusations tied to generational curses.

Key Themes

- **Satan as the Accuser:** Satan operates as a legal complainant in the spiritual realm, accusing believers day and night before God. His accusations are based not only on current sins but also on historical iniquities in the bloodline, which must be addressed to secure spiritual freedom.
- **The Power of Spiritual Tongues:** Voices in the unseen realm form judgments and weapons against believers, creating hindrances in their lives. By targeting and silencing these voices, rather than merely addressing their effects, believers can dismantle the spiritual strongholds they empower.
- **Authority Through Righteousness:** The righteousness of Christ, received as a gift, grants believers the authority to stand in the Courts of Heaven. This position allows them to silence accusations and reclaim their spiritual inheritance as heirs of God's promises.
- **The Role of the Blood of Jesus:** The blood of Jesus is a powerful testimony in the Courts of Heaven, effectively silencing every accusation. When believers invoke the blood, they align with its authority and annul the enemy's legal claims.
- **Cleansing Bloodlines:** Generational curses and unrepented sins in family histories give the accuser grounds to operate. Through repentance and applying the blood of Jesus, believers can cleanse

their bloodlines and remove the legal rights Satan uses against them.

Conclusion

Silencing the voices of accusation is essential to experiencing the fullness of God's kingdom in every area of life. By recognizing their authority in Christ, relying on His righteousness, and applying the blood of Jesus in the Courts of Heaven, believers can condemn every voice raised against them. This spiritual practice enables them to live in freedom, breakthrough, and victory, fulfilling their God-given purposes without hindrance.

CHAPTER 15

SIGNS OF CURSES FROM OUR BLOODLINE

Bible Verse

*"Like a flitting sparrow, like a flying swallow, so a curse
without cause shall not alight."* —Proverbs 26:2
(NKJV)

Introduction

Thischapterexploreshowcurses
originating from bloodline issues operate
as spiritual forces designed to sabotage
success and hinder the fulfillment of God's purposes. By identifying the signs of curses and understanding their legal roots, believers can address
these issues in the Courts of Heaven, revoke Satan's rights, and experience freedom and
restoration.

Word of Wisdom

*"If we can see the legal claim of
curses be annulled, we can see their power
broken." Robert Henderson*

Main Theme

Curses gain legal access to our lives through unaddressed iniquities in our bloodline, manifesting as spiritual blockages. Identifying and revoking these curses through repentance and the authority of Jesus' work on the cross restores us to God's intended blessings.

Key Points

• Curses require a legal right to operate, often rooted in ancestral sin or iniquity.

• Curses are designed to weaken believers, making them vulnerable to defeat.

• Repetitive attacks and aggressive spiritual opposition are common signs of curses.

• Curses often persist despite prayer until their legal rights are addressed.

• Addressing bloodline issues removes the root cause of curses and stops their effects.

• The Courts of Heaven provide a spiritual framework for revoking the legal claims of curses.

Key Themes

• **The Legal Nature of Curses:** Proverbs 26:2 illustrates that curses cannot attach without a cause, often found in bloodline iniquities. By addressing these legal roots, believers can nullify curses and render them powerless.

- **Curses Weaken and Hinder:** Like Balaam's attempted curse on Israel, curses operate to weaken and prevent God's people from succeeding. Their purpose is to diminish spiritual strength and make victory impossible without divine intervention.

- **Repetitive and Aggressive Attacks:** Persistent, overwhelming attacks often indicate the presence of a curse. These unrelenting challenges can create fear and fatigue, but once the legal rights of the curse are removed, the attacks cease, and peace is restored.

- **The Powerlessness of Prayer Alone:** When curses are rooted in legal claims, prayer may seem ineffective until the underlying legal right is addressed. By petitioning the Courts of Heaven, believers can annul these rights and restore the effectiveness of their prayers.

- **The Source of Curses:** Curses often stem from generational issues, like those that plagued Jericho. Addressing these roots, as Elisha did by going to the source of the problem, brings healing and restoration to what the curse has damaged.

Conclusion

Curses that operate through legal rights in our bloodlines can sabotage God's plans for our lives. However, by recognizing their signs and addressing their roots in the Courts of Heaven, believers can revoke these rights and silence the enemy's influence. With the legal claims annulled, the blessings of the Lord can flow freely, restoring peace, victory, and divine purpose.

CHAPTER 16

THE CURSE OF
PREMATURE DEATH

Bible Verse

"With long life I will satisfy him, and show him My salvation." —Psalm 91:16 (NKJV)

Introduction

This chapter explores the spiritual and legal causes of premature death as a curse that can afflict individuals and families. Through examples from Scripture and real-life experiences, it highlights how innocent bloodshed, dishonor, presumption, and unholy practices grant Satan legal rights to cut lives short. The chapter emphasizes repentance and seeking God's intervention through the Courts of Heaven to revoke these rights and claim God's promise of long life.

Word of Wisdom

"The shedding of innocent blood in our history and ancestry opens the legal door for the devil to land the curse of

premature death against us." Robert Henderson

Main Theme

The curse of premature death is often rooted in legal claims stemming from sins, iniquities, and unrepented actions in an individual's bloodline. By addressing these causes through repentance and spiritual intercession, believers can break the curse and restore God's promise of a long and satisfying life.

Key Points

• Innocent bloodshed, including murder and abortion, grants Satan legal rights to operate the curse of premature death.

• Disrespecting the Lord's Supper or failing to honor the body of Christ can open the door to physical weakness, illness, and premature death.

• Presumption before God, such as treating Him or His presence as common, invites judgment and shortens life.

• The dishonor of prophetic authority or divine instruction can bring generational curses, including premature death.

• Unholy supernatural practices, such as strange fire, grant the enemy grounds to cut lives short.

• Repentance and addressing these sins in the Courts of Heaven remove the legal claims of premature death.

. . .

Key Themes

- **The Power of Innocent Bloodshed:**
  Scripture teaches that shedding innocent
  blood opens a door for curses to afflict
  individuals and families. Repentance for
  ancestral sins involving the loss of innocent
  life is essential to remove this legal claim.
- **The Importance of Reverence in
  Communion:** Taking the Lord's Supper
  without proper discernment leads to
  physical consequences, including
  premature death. Honoring both Christ's
  sacrifice and the body of believers protects
  against spiritual and physical harm.
- **Presumption and Holiness:**
  Presumption, whether in approaching God
  casually or engaging in unauthorized
  spiritual practices, invites judgment.
  Treating God as holy and respecting His
  commands safeguards believers from the
  curse of premature death.
- **The Danger of Dishonoring the
  Prophetic:** Disrespecting or ignoring the
  prophetic voice creates generational
  repercussions, including the potential for
  premature death. Recognizing and valuing
  God's messengers aligns believers with His
  protection and blessings.
- **Revoking Legal Claims Through
  Repentance:** Many causes of premature
  death are rooted in legal rights granted to
  the enemy through sin. By repenting for
  personal and ancestral sins, believers can

annul these rights and live under the
promise of long life in God's salvation.

Conclusion

The curse of premature death operates through
legal claims established by sin and iniquity.
Believers are called to identify these root causes,
repent for their own and their bloodline's sins, and
seek God's justice in the Courts of Heaven.
Through God's grace, repentance, and reverence,
they can revoke the enemy's legal rights and claim
the promise of long life and salvation.

CHAPTER 17

REVOKING CURSES THAT SHORTEN LIFESPANS

Bible Verse

"With long life I will satisfy him, and show him My salvation." — Psalm 91:16 (NKJV)

Introduction

This chapter examines the spiritual roots of premature death, emphasizing that personal or ancestral acts can provide legal grounds for such curses. Through repentance and appeal in the Courts of Heaven, believers can revoke these curses and restore God's promise of longevity.

Word of Wisdom

"God is not causing harm; it is the devil exploiting our missteps to claim legal rights of destruction. But in the Courts of

Heaven, we can annul these claims and secure life." Robert Henderson

Main Theme

The chapter explores various actions and attitudes that, according to scripture, may allow the enemy to legally shorten human lifespans, emphasizing that these can be countered through spiritual intercession and legal appeals in the Courts of Heaven.

Key Points

• **Rebellion against God's authority** can directly lead to premature death.

• **Lack of discipline in children** might expose them to life-shortening dangers.

• **Dishonoring parents** can cut one's life short, as this violates a direct commandment with a promise of long life.

• **Strange or profane fire**, or dabbling in forbidden supernatural realms, invites severe repercussions.

• **Presumptuous sins**, where one tests God's patience or commands, can lead to direct judgment.

Key Themes

• **Spiritual Authority and Rebellion:**
  Defiance against God's appointed
  authority, as exemplified by Korah's
  rebellion, can open legal doors for the devil

to enact curses of premature death. Submission to divine and earthly authority is crucial for protection against such claims.

- **Parental Guidance and Child Discipline:** Properly disciplining children protects them from forming habits or behaviors that could spiritually authorize curses. It's a parental duty to provide correction that steers children away from paths that lead to spiritual and physical jeopardy.

- **The Power of Honor:** Honoring one's parents is tied to the promise of a long life. This commandment remains critical throughout one's life, regardless of the parents' actions or behaviors.

- **Consequences of Unholy Practices:** Engaging in unauthorized spiritual practices ("strange fire") can bring about divine judgment or allow demonic forces to claim rights over one's life. It's vital to remain within the bounds of scripturally sanctioned spiritual activities.

- **The Impact of Words and Actions:** Foolish behaviors and careless words can be used against us in the Courts of Heaven. Guarding our speech and actions is essential to maintaining our spiritual defense against premature death.

Conclusion

To live out the fullness of God's promise for longevity and satisfaction, believers must address and rectify any rebellious behaviors, dishonor, and unwise engagements in their lives and bloodlines. By doing so, they can revoke the enemy's legal rights to enact curses of premature death and step into a life marked by divine favor and protection. Through repentance and submission to God's ways, we ensure our words and deeds align with His will, securing a heritage of long life for ourselves and future generations.

CHAPTER 18

FROM DEFENDANT TO JUDGE

Bible Verse

"See, I have removed your iniquity from you, and I will clothe you with rich robes." — Zechariah 3:4 (NKJV)

Introduction

This chapter explores the transformation from being a defendant to a judge in the Courts of Heaven, highlighting how resolving iniquities in our bloodlines allows us to assume a greater role in God's judicial system.

Word of Wisdom

"When the unclean garments were removed, he was made a judge rather than a defendant. This is what judges do." Robert Henderson

Main Theme

Upon cleansing of personal and ancestral sins, believers are elevated from the position of defendants to judges in the spiritual realm, enabling them to influence divine justice not only for themselves but also for their communities and nations.

Key Points

• **Joshua the High Priest's transformation** illustrates moving from a defendant to a judge through spiritual cleansing.

• **Role of a high priest** was to represent the community before God, emphasizing the importance of purity.

• **Accusations from Satan** are based on the filthiness of sin, which keeps believers from their divine roles.

• **Cleansing iniquity** transforms believers, granting them new robes and authority in the spiritual realm.

• **Authority in the Courts of Heaven** involves not just personal representation but also advocating for cultural and national blessings.

Key Themes

• **Spiritual Representation and Authority:** The role of the high priest like Joshua in Zechariah 3:1-7, who represents the community before God, underscores the importance of purity for effective spiritual leadership. Cleansing from iniquity enables such leaders to transition from defendants to authoritative judges in the heavenly courts.

- **Satan's Role in Accusations:** Satan's accusations are aimed at exploiting the iniquities within our bloodlines to hinder our spiritual and communal roles. Understanding and overcoming these accusations are crucial for stepping into a judicial role in the spiritual realm.

- **Transformation Through Cleansing:** The removal of 'filthy garments' symbolizes the purification from sin and iniquity, allowing believers to don new robes of righteousness. This transformation is essential for taking up new roles as judges in the Courts of Heaven.

- **Judicial Authority in the Courts of Heaven:** Once cleansed, believers are not only freed from accusations but are also empowered to govern the spiritual courts. This authority extends to making judicial decisions that impact both individual and communal spiritual realms.

- **Advocacy for Communities and Nations:** As judges in the heavenly courts, believers can influence divine justice for their communities and nations, ensuring that God's blessings and protections are rightfully dispensed. This role amplifies the significance of personal purity, as it affects broader communal and national realms.

Conclusion

In transitioning from a defendant to a judge in the Courts of Heaven, believers must first address and resolve their personal and ancestral iniquities. This chapter elucidates the process and significance of such a transformation, emphasizing that our spiritual cleanliness has profound implications not only for our personal destinies but also for the divine favor upon the communities and nations we represent. Through this elevated role, we are called to administer God's justice and mercy, ensuring that His will is manifested on Earth as it is in Heaven.

D DESTINY IMAGE

Destiny Image is a prophetic Christian publisher dedicated to empowering believers through Spirit-led messages. Our mission is to equip and inspire individuals to fulfill their God-given destinies by providing transformative resources that resonate with the Charismatic and Pentecostal faith.

We specialize in books, blogs, and back cover copies that reflect prophetic insights, dynamic teachings, and testimonies of faith. Our commitment to fostering spiritual growth and kingdom impact makes Destiny Image a beacon for those seeking to deepen their relationship with God and embrace their calling in the power of the Holy Spirit.

Printed in Great Britain
by Amazon

58523763R10046